--- ✦ ---

"My highest ambition lies in excelling in the art.
I pursue it not as a source of gain or
mearly an amusement, I trust that I have
higher aims than these."

—Frederic Church

_____

GEORGE CATLIN. *Black Rock, A Two Kettle (?) Chief, Western Sioux, Teton.*
1832. Oil on canvas, 29" × 24". Smithsonian American Art Museum,
Washington, DC / Art Resource, NY.

COME LOOK WITH ME

Art in Early America

Randy Osofsky

BANK STREET COLLEGE OF EDUCATION

Charlesbridge

Copyright © assigned 2006 to Charlesbridge Publishing

While every effort has been made to obtain permission from the artists and copyright
holders of the works herein, there may be cases where we have been unable to contact a
copyright holder. The publisher will be happy to correct any omission in future printings.

Published by Charlesbridge
85 Main Street
Watertown, MA 02472
(617) 926-0329
www.charlesbridge.com

Originally Published by Lickle Publishing, Inc., 2002.

Library of Congress Control Number
2002104202

ISBN-13: 978-1-890674-12-0; ISBN-10: 1-890674-12-5 (reinforced for library use)

Series producer: Charles Davey
Edited by Bank Street College of Education,
Andrea Perelman, Project manager
Production & Design: Charles Davey *design* LLC
Printed in China

(hc) 10 9 8 7 6 5 4

Contents

Preface

In colonial America and in the first decades of United States history, little commercial demand existed for the fine arts of painting and sculpture. For this reason, much of the art of the period took a variety of other, often utilitarian, forms. Creative expression abounded in media including needlework, architecture, and furniture making. The rich history of these artworks and the people who made them offer insight into the development of the nation itself.

Exploration of the art in *Come Look with Me: Art in Early America* will encourage children to consider history from the perspective of visual culture. No previous knowledge of art history is required to enjoy this book, which will introduce children to artists, art history, and aesthetics through meaningful discussion of compelling works of art. The questions posed with each artwork encourage young people to look closely, analyze, and share their impressions. This engaging approach helps develop language skills and abstract thinking about the elements and principles of art. After investigating the artworks presented in this book, explorations with art materials are encouraged.

How to use this book

COME LOOK WITH ME: Art in Early America is part of a series of interactive art appreciation books for children. Like the other books in the series, this one can be shared with one child or a small group of children. Each of the twelve works of art is paired with a set of questions meant to stimulate thoughtful discussion between adults and children. The accompanying text, which gives background information on the artist and the work, can be read silently or aloud by the adult while the children look at the illustrations.

Ask a child to point to part of the image while he or she discusses it. When working with a group, ask if anyone has a different idea. There are no right or wrong answers to the questions, and everyone will benefit from the different perspectives that experience, age, and personal taste can bring to a group discussion. To keep the interaction lively, it is best to limit each session to the discussion of two or three works of art.

This book can be used in the classroom, at home, and of course, in museums. There is no substitute for a visit to a museum to see the color and texture of an artist's brush strokes and take in the size of an original artwork. However, the methods given here can help children learn a way of looking at original works of art and encourage them to share their understanding with others.

RUFUS HATHAWAY. *Lady with Her Pets (Molly Wales Fobes).*
1790. Oil on canvas, 34¼" × 32". The Metropolitan Museum of Art, Gift of Edgar William and Bernice
Chrysler Garbisch, 1963 (63.201.1). Image © The Metropolitan Museum of Art.

Describe the clothing this woman wears.

What animals do you see in this painting? Why do you think the artist included them?

Do you think that the bird perched on the ring is in front, beside, or behind the woman? What makes you think so?

Artists often use different types of lines to create visual textures. Where in this painting do you see repeated lines? What textures are created by this effect?

If you want a picture of yourself or a friend, you usually get a camera. Before the invention of the camera, people who wanted pictures of themselves or their loved ones hired artists (called "face-painters" or "limners") to paint their portraits. Portrait painting was the most popular art form in early America.

Rufus Hathaway (1770–1822) was one of these face painters. He created *Lady with Her Pets (Molly Wales Fobes)* when he was only twenty years old. The portrait shows eighteen-year-old Molly Wales Fobes with her pet cat and birds. Hathaway developed a distinctive style of portrait painting by using strong colors and flattened surfaces. Even though this painting looks flat, you can see how the artist used overlapping elements to show that some objects were in front of others. You can tell that the cat at the left is behind Molly because part of her skirt is in front of it. You can also tell that Molly's left arm is closer to us than her right one because she is holding it out over her billowing pink skirt.

Hathaway's picture is one of the most famous of what critics called "primitive" portraits done in early America. The word "primitive" was used to indicate that the artist used simple techniques, probably because he or she had not received any artistic training. Despite his supposed lack of such instruction (we don't know for sure), Hathaway became a very successful portrait painter. However, he only painted for five years, from 1790 to 1795, then married and became a doctor.

Painted *Kas*
1700–35. Tulip, maple; painted decoration. 59⅞" × 62¼" × 22⅝". New York, NY.
Courtesy, Winterthur Museum.

Does this cupboard look like something you have in your home? How is it similar to cabinets that you have seen before? How is it different?

What do you notice about the raised decorations on the doors of this cabinet?

Why do you think this cabinet was so extravagantly decorated?

What do you imagine might have been kept in this cabinet?

During the late 1600s and early 1700s, immigrants from European countries began to settle the east coast of North America. (This was well before the colonists won their independence from Great Britain in 1783 and named the area the United States.) They brought with them the artistic styles of their native lands. Although these settlers attempted to carve out new kinds of art forms to go with their new lives, their creations inevitably had roots in the traditions of their original countries.

One art form that is present in every culture involves the decoration of everyday objects. One example is this Dutch-inspired *kas* (a word that in Dutch can mean cupboard, wardrobe, or cabinet). While the maple cupboard was created for a practical purpose, possibly to store linens, it was extensively decorated. Its owners and their guests could thus view the beautiful artwork every day.

To decorate this *kas*, the artist used a painting technique known as *grisaille* (which comes from the French word for gray). He created distinctive images of fruit clusters by using different shades of gray modeled to give a three-dimensional effect to a two-dimensional surface. As a result, the fruit clusters look like a relief, a type of sculpture that rises partway up from a flat surface.

In Colonial times, such cupboards were mostly found in New York and New Jersey, because those areas were extensively settled by the Dutch. New York City itself was once Dutch, and was then called New Amsterdam.

LOUISA H. PLYMPTON. *The Family Record.*
c. 1819. Silk threads and crinkled silk floss on linen (34 threads to the inch).
Satin, tent, Gobelin, Roumanian, and crossstitches, 15¼" × 16". © Mary Jaene Edmonds.

What do you see stitched into this work?

Do you think that one type of stitch was used or a variety of stitches? How long do you think it took to stitch?

What do you think the tree might represent? What do you think the hearts might represent?

If you were to stitch needlework like this, what words and images would you include?

This piece of embroidery is called a sampler; that is, an image sewn using a needle with silk thread. Louisa Plympton, a student at a private boarding school, was only seven years old when she made this family tree.

The sampler was a common art form among schoolgirls in New England, especially those living in northern Massachusetts and southern Maine during the late 1820s. While each sampler was unique, almost all of them shared some common characteristics. For example, most have words cross-stitched in the center and a border consisting of a patterned floral arrangement.

Louisa's sampler is typical of its kind. She has decorated the border with two kinds of flowers separated by green leaves. Before Louisa began sewing, however, her schoolmistress would have drawn the flowers onto the cloth with a pen. Louisa put the heart shapes at the bottom of the tree to symbolize both family and religious love. Although she chose to make the sampler look pretty, her main purpose was to record her family history. Each apple in the sampler represents a child. The apples connected to the tree carry the names of the living children, but the two apples floating in air represent family members no longer alive. By including their names and dates of birth, Louisa made sure that these people would not be forgotten. For art historians, these dates have an added benefit because they help trace the history of this type of embroidery.

---- ✦ ----

Building Interior
What objects do you notice in this room that are from long ago?

How do you think people heated this room during Colonial times? How do you think the room was lit during the day and night?

What do you think people used this room for?

Building Exterior
What shapes do you see in this building?

Describe how the architect arranged the windows and front door.

Does this building look simple and organized or fancy and complicated? What makes you think so?

Samuel McIntire (1757–1811) designed buildings and furniture. He was born in Salem, Massachusetts and lived there his entire life. He learned about architecture from his father and by reading books on building design.

McIntire designed the Gardner-Pingree House in the Federal style. This style was derived from the ancient Romans' architectural ideals for building— using long lines and flat surfaces to organize space. By doing this, the Romans were able to create an ordered balance, or symmetry, in their buildings. The result was a simple, but stately beauty. The third president of the United States, Thomas Jefferson, who designed his own home, admired the Federal style because he felt it proved that the new American republic was similar to the glorious ancient Roman republic.

We can see many elements of the Federal style in the design of the Gardner-Pingree House. It is made of brick, has prominent chimneys, is three stories high, and has windows with panes and wooden shutters. The house also has white columns on either side of the front door, another common Federal feature. These columns make the house look elegant. You can see similar columns today on many government buildings.

McIntire decorated the interior of the Gardner-Pingree House in the plain but refined Sheraton Style. The rooms are spare and uncluttered, with only a sprinkling of paintings, and the furniture has straight lines, graceful proportions and very little decoration.

SAMUEL MCINTIRE.
Gardner-Pingree House.
1805. Second-Floor Study and
View of Front Exterior Looking West.
Photograph Courtesy
Peabody Essex Museum.
Photography by Jeffrey Dykes.

15

SARAH MIRIAM PEALE. *A Slice of Watermelon.*
c. 1825. Oil on canvas, 17" × 21⅞". Wadsworth Atheneum Museum of Art, Hartford, CT.
The Ella Gallup Sumner and Mary Catlin Sumner Collection Fund.

Where in this painting do you see curved lines? Where do you see straight lines?

What is the most noticeable object in the painting? Where did the artist place it?

How does the artist create the illusion of depth?

If you were to paint a still life composed of just one fruit, what fruit would you choose, and why?

Sarah Miriam Peale (1800–85) was born into a family of artists in Philadelphia. Her uncle, Charles Peale, was one of the most important American artists of his time. He believed in the equality of women and encouraged his niece to pursue her artistic talent. As a result, she became a respected and popular portrait painter.

In her portraits, Peale often focused on details, especially the frills and lace on her patron's clothes. Although she made her living as a portrait artist, she also painted landscapes and still lifes. Sarah Miriam Peale was one of two women elected to the Pennsylvania Academy of Fine Arts, and her works were often exhibited in the Academy's gallery. The other woman elected to the Academy was her sister Anna. The two sisters were the first women painters in the United States to receive such a high honor, as well as the first to achieve professional recognition as artists.

In *A Slice of Watermelon*, Peale captures the truth and beauty of a simple subject. The watermelon has been pitted of its seeds, and the holes that are left create an interesting design. This design, together with the melon's bright red and green colors, attracts the viewer's attention—we want to look at the watermelon. The angle of the knife also draws the viewer's eye to the melon. Peale was able to do this by using perspective, that is, creating a sense of three-dimensional depth on the flat canvas. Many other artists of the time could not master this technique

REMBRANDT PEALE. *Three Little Faces.*
1830. Oil on canvas, 28" × 24".
Private Collection / Peter Harholdt / SuperStock.

Where do you see light in this painting? Where do you see shadows?

How does the artist use color to emphasize the faces of the children he depicts?

What might these children be thinking about? Do you think they are content? Why or why not?

Compare Rufus Hathaway's *Lady with Her Pets* (pp. 8 – 9) with this painting. Which looks more realistic to you? Why do you think that is?

Rembrandt Peale (1778–1860) was one of the most well-known and respected artists of the late 1700s and early 1800s. When he was only seventeen, Peale became the youngest artist ever to paint a portrait of George Washington. Peale went on to paint the portraits of many important Americans, including President Thomas Jefferson.

Peale was famous for his use of perspective, a technique he used to make the flat canvas look like a three-dimensional space. As a result, his paintings seem very realistic, almost like photographs. Peale also had the ability to give the viewer a sense of the character and personality of the people he painted, so that they became more than mere figures on a canvas.

In *Three Little Faces*, Peale demonstrates his mastery of portraiture. He presents three beautiful children gazing out at the viewer. Their faces are the focus of the painting. We can't help noticing the rosy red color of their cheeks and lips. This is because Peale made them more noticeable by painting other objects in the picture red as well—the chair behind them and the red fabric they lean on in the foreground. He makes the children appear glowingly angelic by framing their faces with light hair and dressing them in light-colored clothes. The viewer gets the distinct impression that Peale wanted us to see these children as sweet, silent, and obedient—the ideal of the perfect child in the 1800s.

JOHN JAMES AUDUBON. *Great Horned Owl (Bubo virginianus)*.
1814. Watercolor, pastel, graphite on paper, 35⅛" × 24⅞".
Collection of The New-York Historical Society, 1863.17.061

What can you tell about owls from this illustration?

Compare the two owls. What do you notice are the differences between them?

Do you think the birds in this illustration look realistic? Why or why not?

If you were to create an illustration of one kind of bird, what bird would you choose and why?

In 1820, after he had failed in all his business ventures, including working as a taxidermist (someone who stuffs dead animals to exhibit them), twenty-year-old John James Audubon (1785–1851) decided to pursue his dream of creating pictures of all the birds of America.

To finance this large task, Audubon first traveled to Europe, where he was able to get subscribers—people who agreed to pay him in advance for the pictures he would make. By 1838, Audubon had drawn 435 birds. He considered each illustration to be not only a record of what a particular species looked like, but a work of art in itself. Audubon then wrote *Birds of America*, a book describing the habits of these birds.

To share his birds with the world, Audubon made many copies of his artwork, using a process by which he could transfer his pictures onto pieces of metal called plates. These plates could print a picture the same way many times.

This plate shows the Great Horned Owl, a predatory bird that hunted at night and was found mostly in Ohio and Mississippi. Audubon fits both the male and the female owl into the small space of the picture by placing one in front of the other. The owl's large eyes show the bird's fierceness; the way in which its ears point up show how alert it is. In his writings, Audubon described this owl as graceful and powerful, qualities he attempted to depict in this illustration.

FREDERIC CHURCH. *Cotopaxi, Ecuador.*
Copy attributed by some art historians to DeWitt Clinton Boutelle. 1862. Oil on canvas, 35" × 60".
Courtesy of the Reading Public Museum, Reading, PA.

Which are the lightest areas of this painting? Which are the darkest?

Do you think that the sun is rising or setting? What makes you think so?

What effect does the light have on the mood of this painting? How do the colors affect the mood of this painting?

How do you think this artist felt about the environment he painted?

Frederic Church (1826–1900), one of the most important American landscape painters of the nineteenth century, possessed an amazing ability to depict light and color. He used these skills in order to paint very beautiful and realistic landscapes.

Church belonged to a movement known as the "Hudson River School," a group of American painters who focused on painting beautiful pictures of landscapes in the United States. These painters were especially attracted to the scenery of the Hudson River Valley region in upstate New York. Church himself created many paintings of the Catskill mountains in this same region. However, he was particularly interested in the wonders of nature, such as icebergs, waterfalls, tropical forests, and volcanoes.

Church's picture, *Cotopaxi, Ecuador*, depicts the Cotopaxi volcano in central Ecuador, a country on the west coast of South America. The artist uses rich colors to present the volcano's eruption at sunset. True to his membership in the Hudson River School, Church takes care to emphasize the beauty of nature in this work. At the bottom of the painting, a small waterfall includes a rainbow of colors. The volcano itself seems unusually calm, considering that it is erupting. The smoke spewing from the volcano, instead of overpowering the rest of the painting, adds a gentle, rich red to the sunset, thus making the scene look even more beautiful.

The picture became so popular that Church painted many copies of it. Under pressure to produce prints of the painting, Church's publisher authorized the artist DeWitt Clinton Boutelle to produce a copy. Church retouched the painting to maintain his high standards. Art historians disagree about whether the painting shown here is by Church or Boutelle.

GEORGE CATLIN. *Black Rock, A Two Kettle (?) Chief, Western Sioux, Teton.*
1832. Oil on canvas, 29" × 24". Smithsonian American Art Museum,
Washington, DC / Art Resource, NY.

Describe the man, Chief Black Rock, who stands in the center foreground of this painting.

Describe what you see in the background of the painting.

What role does color play to help accentuate details in Chief Black Rock's clothing?

Why do you think the artist painted this picture of Chief Black Rock?

From the time he was a small child, George Catlin (1796–1872) was fascinated by the cultures of American Indians. Part of this was the result of his mother's stories of being captured by the Iroquois when she was seven years old. Although he studied to become a lawyer like his father, in 1823 Catlin decided to become a portrait artist instead. By 1829, he was already using his self-taught painting skills to record his observations of many groups of American Indians. From 1837 to 1845, he created and exhibited more than 500 paintings and sketches of them. In 1841, Catlin published a book of his illustrations, which also contained detailed descriptions of the customs of the cultures he had observed.

This particular painting is of Black Rock, a Chief of the Western Sioux. Catlin emphasizes the man's high status by focusing on his elaborate headdress, with its horns and long eagle feathers, as well as on the lavishly decorated robes he wears. His high status is also evident from the way Catlin has placed him in the picture. Artists often borrow from the paintings of the past. Here, Catlin has Chief Black Rock stand before us in a pose that resembles those of Roman Senators depicted in antique art. Catlin further emphasizes Black Rock's importance by providing the viewer with a sharp contrast between the dramatic colors he uses for the chief's headdress and robes and the faint colors with which he paints the subtle background of the Western Sioux village.

MARTIN JOHNSON HEADE. *Thunder Storm on Narragansett Bay.*
1868. Oil on canvas, 32⅛" × 54¾".
Amon Carter Museum, Fort Worth, Texas. 1977.17.

How would you describe the colors in this seascape?

In what way does the texture of the water differ from the texture of the clouds?

What mood has the painter created in this work of art?

What might the people in this scene be thinking? What might they be feeling?

Martin Johnson Heade (1819–1900) received very little artistic training as a youth in rural Pennsylvania. However, he later studied art in Europe and traveled widely in Brazil and America. Heade never settled for long in any one place, but he painted landscapes and seascapes wherever he went. Like Frederic Church (pp. 22 – 23), Heade was a member of the Hudson River School. Over the years, Heade developed such a fine artistic style that his work is greatly appreciated today.

Heade's *Thunder Storm on Narragansett Bay*, painted near Bristol, New Hampshire, is one of his best seascapes. He depicts the storm that is looming overhead as both violent and beautiful by using dark and dramatic colors. He adds to the drama of the scene by his use of contrast between the dark and light colors in this painting. In the top right of the picture, Heade shows us the dark sky full of storm clouds. In the bottom left, he depicts the bay as it normally looks, light and serene. The water itself is clear and still, providing an almost mirror-like reflection of the sailboats in the bay.

Art historians had forgotten about this painting until the 1940s. When it was rediscovered, the critics all agreed that Heade was a great artist. This particular painting is an excellent example of how this artist used "panoramic" design, that is, how he painted with a wide view to include as much scenery as possible on the canvas.

THOMAS CHAMBERS. *Capture of H.R.M Frigate* Macedonian *by U.S. Frigate* United States, *October 25, 1812.*
1852. Oil on canvas. 30¾" x 50¼". Smithsonian American Art Museum, Washington, DC.
Gift of Sheldon and Caroline Keck in honor of Elizabeth Brown / Art Resource, NY.

Describe the textures you see in the clouds, the waves, and the smoke coming from the ship.

How can you tell that the two ships are battling?

Which is the American ship? How do you know?

Describe the condition of the two ships in the moment depicted in this painting. Which ship seems to be winning the battle?

Thomas Chambers (1808–66?) was born in England and moved to the United States in 1832. He is considered a member of the Hudson River School because, despite his English heritage, he was a patriotic American who painted many famous landscapes and seascapes.

Chambers did not visit every place he painted. He used his imagination to paint what he thought the scenes probably looked like, or else he used images he saw in popular prints of the time.

Chambers based his *Capture of the H.R.M. Frigate* Macedonian *by the U. S. Frigate* United States, *October 12, 1812* on a print of this famous battle that occurred during the War of 1812, which was fought between England and America. In it, an American ship captures a British ship. The picture could also be called a historical painting because it shows an event that actually happened.

However, Chambers' technique in this painting was not very realistic. The ocean waves, the billowing smoke, and the ships themselves don't look very real. But Chambers succeeds in portraying the excitement and drama of the battle with his use of bright colors and repetitious patterns. The artist also shows how tense the fighting is with details like bullet holes in the sails of both ships and the huge clouds of gun smoke rolling across the water. The American flag flapping in the wind reminds us that this battle was fought for America.

UNKNOWN. *The* Ohio Star *Buggy.*
c. 1850. Daguerreotype, sixth plate. 2¾" x 3¼".
Smithsonian American Art Museum, Washington, DC / Art Resource, NY.

Describe the scene shown in this early photograph.

Because of the way people and objects are placed in the scene, what do you think the photographer wanted us to notice first?

Who do you think these people might be? What do you think the horse and buggy were used for?

Do you think the early photograph is a more accurate depiction of the scene than a painting would be? Why or why not?

An important influence on early American art was the invention of photography. Two Frenchmen, Louis-Jacques-Mandé Daguerre and Joseph-Nicéphore Niépce, developed an early form of it during the 1830s. They named their technique after Daguerre: Daguerreotype. It was a complicated and expensive process that involved using chemicals to fix an image onto a copper plate.

Nobody knows who made *The* Ohio Star *Buggy* daguerreotype. We do know that the buggy in the image was used to deliver the *Ohio Star* newspaper to its readers. In those days, this was a new way to distribute papers. That the *Ohio Star* could afford to be distributed in this way tells us that the newspaper was successful.

We see here only one of the many uses of daguerreotypes in the 1800s. People also purchased daguerreotypes of artworks, architectural views, and outdoor scenes. The great majority of daguerreotypes were portraits. Many Americans were more than happy to pay the price for such pictures of their family members.

Eventually, cheaper and less complex photographic techniques were developed. Photographs then became an important and increasingly common alternative to painted portraits. As it increased in popularity, photography expanded the recording of American life that was originally only possible through paintings. Today our options for recording our lives have increased to include digital, movie, and video cameras.

Go back and look through these pages again.

Which of the artworks would you like to have in your home?

Which one looks the most simplistic?

Which one looks the most realistic?

What do you think the painters in this book would paint if they were alive today?

On a different day, answer these questions again. You may see things you missed before. You may also see things you saw before in a different way.

Keep looking!